LIFE, LIBERTY, AND THE PURSUIT OF

Purpose

COLLEGE BOY
PUBLISHING
"We Breed Bestsellers"

Women in Business/Entrepreneurship/Self-Help/Spirituality

ISBN: 978-1-944110-39-0

Edited by **Armani Valentino & LaTangela Vann**
for College Boy Publishing
Published for Print and Digital formats by **Armani Valentino** for
College Boy Publishing
Cover Design by **Armani Valentino**
for College Boy Publishing
Cover photos by:
Written by **Ulanda Arnett**

Published in Dallas, TX, by College Boy Publishing, LLC.
College Boy Publishing is a division of The College Boy Company & ArmaniValentino.com. To order *wholesale or bulk orders* of this book, please contact the publisher directly at collegeboypublishing@gmail.com or call 972-781-8404.

Autographed copies of this book may be ordered directly from
www.UlandaArnett.com

Please allow up to 7-14 Business Days for delivery.

Ulanda Arnett is available for keynote addresses, speaking engagements workshops, panel discussions, consultations, and radio & television interviews please contact her at **arnettu@gmail.com** or **@Prettypurposefullady** on *Instagram.*

Printed in the United States of America

08 09 10 11 12 UAAV 5 4 3 2 1

LIFE, LIBERTY, AND THE PURSUIT OF
Purpose

WRITTEN BY

Wanda Arnett

Dedication

This book is dedicated to my Grandma Cole…the matriarch that birthed a long line of passionate, smart, and hard-working children. She was a humble, compassionate woman who taught me the value of education, hard work, and faith in God.

Grandma Cole

April 15, 1929 – March 8, 2018.

Life Liberty, and The Pursuit of Purpose

This Is For The Dreamer

This is for the Dreamer

The one that knows there is something greater

The one that has faith that the BEST is coming later

That stands again in the face of failure

That pursues their passion in the midst of tests

That resilient one that just won't rest.

This is for the Vision Aire

The one that can see things before they're there

That falls seven times, but stands up eight

The one that knows inside there's something great

That one that sees their future at the top

And until they get there just won't stop.

This is for the Trailblazer

The one willing to go where no one has gone.

That one that makes testing the limits their home.

That consistently steps outside their comfort zone.

That one that longs to live on purpose.

That keeps their pursuit as their major focus.

This is for the Risk Taker.

The one that's not afraid to move, be a shaker.

That's known as a difference maker.

A barrier breaker.

That has the courage to stand alone.

Stand for right, and not wrong.

This is for the Leader.

The one known as a serial believer.

That trust God to be an overachiever.

That is a knowledgeable consumer & retriever.

That has faith in God.

Even when it's against all odds.

Yes, this is for you.

May all your dreams come true.

May God Bless all you do…

As you pursue…

Purpose.

With Love,

Ulanda

THE PURSUIT OF

Purpose

What would you do if you could do anything without failing?

What would you do if you could do anything without failing?

That's a pretty powerful question, huh? It's one of the questions that helped me take the leap and pursue my side hustle full-time. Are you at a place in life where you feel there is a higher, greater calling for your skills and talents? Do you dread going to your 8 -5 job? Is getting ready for work in the morning depressing? Do you get the blues on Sunday evening but super excited on Friday when it's time for the weekend? I used to look forward to leaving work during the week and going home for the weekend. It was a classic case of living for the weekend.

One day I ran into one of the Chaplains at my previous corporate employer of almost 12 years. I was on a mission to check some things off my to-do list for the day, so I had no plans of talking to anyone, let alone having a conversation on a deep level. During our talk, she really hit home when she used the analogy that sometimes God makes things uncomfortable for us just like the parents of eagles when the eaglets are ready to fly; they put rocks in the nest to make them uncomfortable. This analogy really resonated with me.

I was working a role that provided a steady paycheck, benefits, and a great annual bonus.

However, rarely did I feel empowered, let alone challenged. I knew I was not living or working up to my full potential. And for some reason, I felt stuck.

My family was very proud of me working a 6 -figure job for a Fortune 100 company. Most people associated my professional brand with that company. Over the years, I had become very involved in the community representing the company on several boards and associations. I asked myself time and time again, "Are you really ready to walk away."; to rebuild your professional brand. My personal life was blooming the way I had always envisioned as well.

My ex-husband and I had recently built our dream home (on 2 acres of land next to a stocked pond), and I had purchased my dream car about a year before. We owned over 1 million in real estate with our current home and several rental properties. So, when would be the perfect time to leave my job? If I was honest with myself, I never felt I was fully prepared to step out and become a full-time entrepreneur.

There was always something saying stay for one more bonus, save more money, plan for this much more time before you leave your corporate job.

Personally, an even deeper question challenged me...Who Am I? That's a great question. But it was one I couldn't answer for a while in my mid-thirties. On the outside looking in, I had what some would classify as all: a six-figure salary, a million-dollar home, a luxury car, beautiful kids, and a handsome husband. I was living "the life," but the soul biopsy inspired by entrepreneurship forced me to deal with every area in my life truthfully...

ARE YOU HOLDING YOUR BREATH OR ARE YOU

Breathing

Are You Holding Your Breath, Or...

Are You Breathing?

I felt stuck until this life changing question forced me to reprioritize what was important to me and how I defined success. It simply was, "Are you holding your breath, or are you breathing?" I knew then my mind and habits were not at their best because it was time for a new, challenging yet purposeful chapter. Two days later, I turned in my 2-week notice to my corporate employer. Now what?

Pursuing my side hustle full-time required me to connect to my passion, clarify my purpose, and commit to a strategic plan. All that sounded logical and great until REAL life issues started to affect my confidence and the way I approached becoming a full-time entrepreneur.

Even though the choice to walk away from my corporate job happened relatively quickly after hearing that life-changing question, I had been planning and preparing myself and my family for the job transition long before that. If I was going to walk away from a pretty plush job at a top growing company to pursue my passion full-time, there were several things I needed to make sure were in order.

Most things we see about entrepreneurship are the glamorous side. We usually see the fruits of the labor of the business owners after years of sacrifice, problem-solving, and very hard work. But there is another side of the entrepreneurial journey that can be filled with sacrifice and uncertainty.

So why would a sane person leave a stable, reputable company, and six-figure job to start a company from scratch and risk everything that they and their family had worked for many years. It had to be a compelling case. The pursuit of purpose. God-given purpose.

I

START WITH THE
Why

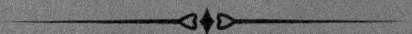

"When you start with WHY, those who believe what you believe are drawn to you for very personal reasons. It is those who share your values and beliefs, not the quality of your products, that will cause the system to tip."

~Simon Sinek~

What are you after? What is your purpose for living? How do you define happiness? For me, happiness is living my highest best purpose that aligns with God's will for my life.

Three primary reasons stood out to me on why entrepreneurship was the best professional route for:

1. Working at my highest (best use) with my unique abilities and God-given gifts

2. Living life on my terms (more flexibility with how much I work)

3. Leaving a Legacy and inheritance for my family

If your business is about meeting a need and helping others by providing a product or a service, you have to remind yourself of your "why" constantly. You must cling to the WHY that prompted you to be a full-time entrepreneur. This WHY helps motivate you at times when you may get discouraged. Statistics show that most small businesses last an average of three years. Most struggle with funding, marketing, and making enough to sustain fulltime. After about 2.5 years into my full-time journey, I didn't want to become another statistic.

Most of the people stepping out into the entrepreneurship journey believe there is something greater than they have to offer the world.

Whether it's a unique product or service, they believe they have the tenacity to step out on faith. It encourages me that one of the fastest-growing demographics of entrepreneurs is black women. "Despite institutional barriers that disproportionately separate black women from venture capital, black women's entrepreneurial strength is growing at a higher rate than any other groups of women." (The Nielsen Company).

I knew if I waited for the perfect time to leave my corporate job that I would never make the move. The pay was great, the benefits were excellent, & the stability gave me comfort when planning my expenses. My bonus percentage had just increased to 1/3 of my salary. I kept thinking it could be good seed money to get my business going. I was also aware of the ***Law of Diminishing Intent. It states "the longer you wait to do something you should do now, the greater the odds that you will never actually do it."***

My "purpose goals" helped me define my "WHY." Purpose goals are the overarching goals you want to define your life…it is the dash between your birth date and your death date. When you think of it this way, it makes you want to take it more seriously.

It's simple; what do you want to be known for?

Here are my purpose goals:

1. Working and making a difference with the unique talents and abilities that God has blessed me.
2. Helping others recognize their unique God-given abilities and purpose.
3. Building and enjoying an impactful empire.
4. Raising children that are kind, productive, and strong in their Christian beliefs.
5. Donating to non-profits and people in need.

6. Living an abundant, prosperous, and long life with a Christian, loving spouse.

My Truth

Everything was "peachy" at the beginning of my entrepreneurship journey. My "Why" was clear. My family appeared to be on board. My excitement and drive were at an ultimate high. Friends and family were ready to support me in my new endeavor. Everyone was ready to cutback and modify our lifestyle until we were over the "new business hump."

A few months passed, and a lot of my initial excitement was challenged. I found it hard to find a balance between marketing my business and being pushy about selling my products & services. I didn't have a business loan, so all the funding was coming from me.

My overhead costs were way too high. If I'm honest, I started with lots of drive and ambition. Eventually, I found myself playing it safe and small because I could. I had money saved, so I always relied on it as my cushion. About two years in, I got more aggressive began taking risks and purchased two buildings back in my hometown. I paid cash for them, which at the time seemed like a good idea. Looking back, I should have saved as much of my cash as possible, and got a business loan for business transactions.

In a corporate environment, so much is based on how much "self-initiative" you take. It's all about strategy, execution, and professional development. All of those are very important for entrepreneurship as well, but it takes a type of mental toughness that most can only develop from actually experiencing it.

Lesson Learned: I found myself making it-relying on my strength. Until "my strength" only took me so far, and I knew I had to make a "shift" if I was going to make it. It had to be more than just mental. I needed Jesus to be "my guide" …spiritually, mentally, and physically.

Purpose

Oh how sweet it is to know

That one purpose that is yours for sho

That of all the people on this earth

You were given this assignment before birth

Oh how humbling it is to see

That all things

are working for me

The good, the bad, the ugly, the great

The crooked, the curves, the upright, the straight

Oh how great it is to hear

That my faith triumphs my fear

The lessons, the losses, the gains, the wins.

The blessings, the miracles, the shames, the sins

Oh how awesome it is to feel

A love and passion so real

That can make a difference with mankind

When your true calling you find

Thank you for your grace

And reminding me why I was made

No matter how big or small

I will look forward to the call...

Because love conquers ALL!

II

IDENTIFY YOUR

Passion

(THE PURPOSE)

"Where there is passion,
there is love."
~Unknown~

Passion

(your

heart)

So, you have this idea, this skill, or this talent that you are good at doing. It's something that keeps showing up because you are subconsciously drawn to it. You would do it for free if you could.

Have you ever been in love before? If you have, you feel free…liberated. There is nothing you think you can't accomplish. You feel motivated and inspired to achieve your highest good. Most likely, that person inspires you to be more passionate about being your authentic self.

It is the same when identifying your passion for your business. Passion helps fuel your creativity and is vital when starting your own business. There will be many obstacles that will give you all the reasons why it won't work. Passion is that thing that tells you that it will work despite the odds.

"Passion gives you an advantage over others because one person with passion is greater than ninety-nine who have only an interest!"
~John Maxwell~

- What do you enjoy doing so much that you would do it for free?

- What do you find yourself doing in your free time and on weekends?

- What do friends and family tell you that you are great at doing?

- What is your highest best use?

- What is your personal and professional mission?

- What do you want to be famous for?

- What do you want your legacy to be?

- What makes you feel alive?

Once you know your passion, your purpose can align with it. Create a purpose statement to summarize your reason and let it serve a litmus test on where you should and should not focus your energy. You have identified your passion, now what?

You must align your passion with your purpose.

Here are a few examples of purpose statements:

"To build confidence and enhance the beauty in every client that sits in my chair and grace them with the talent that God gave me to make them feel absolutely amazing, beautiful, and pretty."

~Tasha Bradley, Stylist and Owner of Onpointstylin

To motivate, encourage, and inspire others to recognize their God-given purpose, talents, and passion while doing intentional things with the hope of making a positive difference.

~Ulanda Arnett, Posh Inspirations

A few other qualifying questions to help give you clarity are:

How will this opportunity aid you in fulfilling your purpose?

What does your gut tell you to do?

Does this opportunity allow you to work as your highest best self on Earth?

My Truth

To whom much is given, much is required. So, what do you do when you have a passion for many things? This was my dilemma...still is my dilemma today. I have a passion for many things. The good news, I'm not afraid to try new things. The bad news, I'm not afraid to try new things. The challenge for me has been how do you balance each talent while striving to become an expert & skilled at it. A parable about multiplying our talents is shared in the book of Matthew Chapter 25.

God blesses us with many gifts & talents. The challenging part for me has been knowing which talents to focus on primarily. Many people ask questions to find out what talents and side-hustles to turn into a business. I don't have a magic formula on how to know what to focus on first.

Some will say pick one thing and do it very, very well. Others will say diversify...have a few different things so you can have more stability upfront. I choose the latter. The benefit has been slow steady growth in many areas...so when it is slow in one area, I'm able to put more focus on another. The challenge when you have a business offering various products and services has been creating a clear, consistent brand, and knowing how to target the right customers with the right message, so they understand clearly everything that you do.

Leo Buscaglia states, ***"Your talent is God's gift to you. What you do with it is your gift back to God."***

Lesson Learned: It's critical to be passionate about and love whatever profession you choose. If you love what you do, you will never truly work a day in your life. You can do anything and be successful with God's help. One ounce of favor from God can take you further quicker and faster than anyone can ever imagine.

Passion

In a world that tells me to work from my head

I'm just trying to pursue from my heart

Remember it's about where you end

Not so much about where you start

In a world that tells me to only follow the money

I'm working to pursue God's plan

Remember the ultimate goal is eternal life

Not just living to please man

We can be the change

If we step out our range

We can inspire change

If we're not too scared to be strange

III

BUILDING & MAINTAINING
Your Brand

(THE PLAN)

"Branding is the art of aligning what you want people to think about your business with what people actually do think about your business. And vice-versa."

Jay Bear

Plan

(your

head)

We used to ask in the corporate world, "What do you want to be famous for?" I learned quickly that everything counts because everything communicates. Your brand becomes the voice that speaks for you when you are not in the room. We each have a brand, whether we know it or not. It is no exception when it comes to business.

When we think about the brands that we are most loyal to, usually, it's because we have a strong connection to the brand. They have done an effective job communicating who they are and what their product or service stands for. A few of my favorites include Chick-fil-A, Hobby Lobby & Disney World. One thing these businesses do well is tailored customer service. They may not get every order or every interaction perfect, but they usually provide a great customer experience.

Everyone on your team is a representative of your brand. This can be one of the most difficult areas to master as your team grows.

Whatever your passion may be, in order to turn it into an impactful business, ask yourself:

Is it new?

Is it different?

Is it the best?

Your brand strategy helps create a clear, consistent message that articulates who your business is and who it is not. Branding and marketing help connect you with your target market.

Your brand strategy should identify:

Who is your target market?

Where do you find them?

How to market to them?

As a Christian, one of the best ways to find and connect with potential customers has been praying for the right customers at the right time. It amazes me how a simple request to God can yield the customers that we want for our products and/or services.

Networking has its advantages as well. There is usually some type of interest group that sponsors a conference or hosts regular meetings to keep professionals connected and updated on the latest trends in our chosen industry. Social media has proven to be an effective platform to market and connect with current & potential customers. Facebook and Instagram have made finding and connecting with others with similar interests simple. The paid ads on both platforms give you detailed demographics of your target audience.

One of the most effective ways to connect with new customers is to ask your friends & family to share various advertisements & flyers that you post. Most people trust their close social media connections. This makes them more likely to try a service or product that is recommended.

As a small business owner, your business brand matters. However, your brand who you are in Christ is just as important. I mentioned earlier how I never really was able to define myself in my mid-thirties. If you asked me who I was, I probably would have said a wife, mother, sister, aunt, friend, corporate professional, community ambassador, etc.

All those roles were true. My God-given identity became more evident once I was able to define myself not just based on a role or material possessions. I've learned that my identity in Christ stays the same regardless of my job or profession.

Get a Business Plan

Sample One Page Business Plan (on next page)

BUSINESS PLAN
THE ONE PAGE PLAN

DATE: _____

NAME _____

WHY AM I STARTING THIS BUSINESS?

HOW?

WHAT?

CUSITOMER PROBLEM OR NEED I PLAN TO SOLVE?

WHAT'S MY **TARGET MARKET**?

BUSINESS SOLUTION?

WHAT'S MY
COMPETITIVE ADVANTAGE?

TOP 3 GOALS

1.

2.

3.

TOP 3 COMPETITORS

1.

2.

3.

ABC's of a Child of God
(Brand Identity)

I AM Anointed
I AM Blessed
I AM Committed
I AM Determined
I AM Enough
I AM Faithful
I AM Graced
I AM Happy
I AM Inspiring
I AM Justified
I AM Kind
I AM Loved
I AM a Magnet for Miracles
I AM Nice
I AM an Overcomer
I AM Powerful
I AM a Queen
I AM Redeemed
I AM Saved
I AM Thankful
I AM Unique
I AM Verified
I AM Winning
I AM X-tra Special
I AM Zestful

IV

---◆---

MAINTAINING A WINNER'S
Mindset
(THE PLAN)

---◆---

"*A boss is a mindset, not a title.*"

Ulanda Arnett

Plan (your head)

So, as a man thinketh, so is he (Proverbs 23:7)

So, who do you think you are? No really?

I've found that we can be our own biggest obstacle when it comes to having a winner's mindset. Often, we subconsciously or consciously delay pursuing our dreams because we are afraid of failure and not having EVERYTHING we need to get started. EVERYTHING you need is already inside of you. There is no such thing as the PERFECT time to launch a business. If we wait until everything aligns perfectly, we may never start that business. Now I'm not saying you shouldn't create a business plan or a financial and personal strategy before you leave your job. The bills won't stop coming just because you quit working. Of course, we must have financial means to make it in life.

It's critical to know how to rebound after a setback. One technique that has helped me put things into perspective and try not to stress out over things I can't control is the Time Tell Test. I call it the Time Tell Test because most things that we stress over end up not having a significant effect on us over time. When they happen, it seems like the worst thing? I now ask will this situation affect me five months from now, five days from now, or five minutes from now. If the answer is no, then let it go.

One of my favorite quotes is life is 10% of what happens to you and 90% of how you respond. When life happens (things we can't control or haven't planned for), it's all about how we respond. I found it super easy to maintain a winner's mindset when things are peachy, going well, and working in my favor. The litmus test asks how we respond when things don't go our way or are not moving as quickly as we hope. I continuously remind myself that building a successful business is a process that takes LOTS of patience and flexibility.

Even though each business is unique, the process for starting and growing a business is generally the same. One can't cheat the process. In a culture of quick fixes and instant gratification, patience can be a hard virtue to develop, maintain, and master. This is where your mindset plays such a critical role. How do you maintain a winner's mindset when things don't move as quickly as you would like?

Here are a few things that have helped me:

- View each delay or failure as a learning experience. Either I win or I learn. Either way, it's preparing you for the next level. Look at failures as moving you closer to your goals. We call it FAILING FORWARD in the business world.
- It's important to know who you are. If you don't, others will try to define this for you.

If you're anything like me, your self-perspective may change or evolve, but some non-negotiables and basic values remain the same.

• Embrace each stage of the process. The beginning stage of any process can be uncomfortable. Most of us quit at the first sign of opposition. I have found that being an entrepreneur is a lot about problem-solving...how can we use the unique skills and talents that God has blessed us with to make a positive difference in the lives of others.

One tool that has been instrumental in helping me visualize the life I want and maintain a winning mindset is a Vision Board. A Vision Board is a visualization tool, usually a board that you create a collage of words and pics that represent your goals and dreams. I typically create a vision board at the beginning of the year and do regular check-ins to modify and edit the board as things change.

I believe everyone should have a vision board because of the following four reasons:

• Vision boards help provide clarity around what you want and do not want.

• Vision boards help motivate you to progress continually.

- Vision boards help remind you daily of your dreams and goals.

- Vision boards align with the law of manifestation.

- Vision boards can help you refine and define your brand and, most importantly, what it is not.

"Live the Life of your Dreams: Be brave enough to live the life of your dreams according to your vision and purpose instead of the expectations and opinions of others." ~Roy T. Bennett~

Along with my mindset, I often check my words. There may be times in our journey where we may find ourselves discouraged. Each season has a purpose. Some slow seasons are preparation to propel us to one of the greatest seasons & victories in our life. We must learn how to use words that speak LIFE and work for us instead of using words that work against ourselves and others.

As entrepreneurs, our work is very personal. This profession requires us to be reflective of ourselves and deal with our issues so our work will not suffer. It can be difficult to perform at our highest and best use if we are still holding on to mistakes, past hurts, and insecurities. Continually renewing our mind is vital to tap into our God-given purpose.

My Truth

I can't tell you how many times I struggled with maintaining a winner's mindset. When I started, I found myself complaining about how hard of a feat being a full-time entrepreneur really is. There were times that I considered seriously going back into a 9 am – 5 pm job. I missed the steady pay, bonuses, consistent interaction with a designated team, and the predictability of a corporate job. If I called in sick, I still got paid. If I went on vacation, I still got paid. Depending on your business as a full-time entrepreneur, if you don't work, you may not get paid. If you are truly doing what you are called to do, you will find a way to make it work. Most of the battle is in our heads. If you have taken the time to refine and develop a solid product and or service, the ultimate goal is how your product or service can solve a problem for the customer that is looking for this type of solution. In order to think clearly and effectively, you cannot allow negative thoughts to take up space in your head. This means we must change the way we look at failure, rejection, and setbacks.

Lesson Learned: It's difficult to live a productive life with negative thinking. I am enough with GOD. I have everything I need inside of me to succeed when I align my plans with God's purpose for my life, and I'm not afraid to ask others for help.

Who is She?

Who is She?

She is You. She is Me.

A Queen…never anxious for anything

For she knows what her worth & purpose means.

Who is She?

She is You. She is Me.

A Warrior & Fighter…it's a higher power that ignites her.

Her faith in God takes her higher.

Who is She?

She is You. She is Me.

She is a Leader…

not bound by how others may see her.

She is in love with God and considered a leader.

Who is She?

She is You. She is Me.

A Believer… a Truth Seeker. A Life Speaker.

Who is She?

She is You. She is Me.

A Winner…a Saved Sinner.

Growing & Glowing from inner.

It's not just WHO she is, but WHOSE she is!!

Unapologetically Brilliant...

Imperfect but Worthy of Real Love…

Bold…

Beautiful…

Blessed & Highly Favored…

She is ME!!!

V

AVOID

Distractions

"*Most distractions do not show up as distractions until they have already distracted you.*"

~Unknown~

Plan

(your

head)

Remember that when you are your "own" boss, no one is there to hold you accountable for showing up to work from 8-5 pm. There are no regularly scheduled performance appraisals. Your customers become your boss, and their reviews are your feedback for your performance.

Just as it's a force that wants you to fulfill your purpose and life's mission, another force is working against you. This negative force shows up in the form of misconceptions, fake supporters, and personal and professional missteps. It is up to YOU to recognize and OVERCOME these challenges and distractions. Remember, most distractions don't show up as distractions until they have distracted you.

They usually show up as the very thing you are longing or wanting. That's why the spirit of discernment is so important in business. Not everyone or everything is for you!! You may be surprised by how many family members or friends that will support you publicly but talk negative about your business privately. Some call them "haters." If you spend your time focusing on what your "haters" say about you, you could lose focus on your purpose. We are not in business to be liked but to fulfill and/or meet a need. We are in business for the reasons we outlined as our "why."

I found that there are forces that are rooting and aiding you as well. As a believer in Christ, the Holy Spirit has unimaginable power to do the unexpected and cause everything to work in our favor. I've been encouraged and motivated by other entrepreneurs that are willing to share resources and advice to pay it forward to up and coming business owners.

Serenity Prayer

"God grant me the serenity to accept the things I cannot change.

The courage to change the things I can.

And the wisdom to know the difference."

The serenity prayer is one of my favorite mantras. It helps me focus on controlling the controllables and having the courage to change what I can control and not worry about what I cannot control.

Here are a few things that I can control that have helped me minimize the distractions:

- **Early morning devotionals.** Instead of picking up my phone and checking Facebook, Instagram, or emails, I start my day with a morning devotional. During this time, I read my Bible, pray & worship God. This time has been so impactful to my life that now I usually wake before my alarm clock. It has inspired me to crave that time with God and helps set the tone for the rest of my day.

- **Reframing negative comments**. Many people trust me with their concerns and issues. I started noticing my ability to help friends and family see the positive lesson in what may be viewed as a negative situation. As I grew closer to God, I understood how important reframing negative comments are in helping me reach my destiny. The more I was grateful for everything that was going well in my life, the more good things I began to generate.

- **Spending time alone**. I used to think I always had to be around someone in order to feel content. However, the more I craved to get to know me, the more I enjoyed spending time alone. During this time, I self-reflect on what I can do differently to make my life more purposeful. Good soulful gospel and R&B music have helped me grow and deal with many things as well.

- **Having fun**. Sometimes in life, we get so focused on achieving goals and making a living that we may forget to have fun. I noticed that joy and contentment couldn't be found in simple encounters throughout the day.

- **Connect with a tribe that has similar beliefs**. Your tribe will have your best interest in mind. They support you and are happy when things are going well in your life. This group encourages you to do and be your best.

HOW to OVERCOME?

- **Be intentional!** Watch what you feed your mind and what you listen to. These things feed into our behavior, and ultimately our habits.

- *"Watch your thoughts; for they become words. Watch your words; for they become actions. Watch your actions; for they become habits. Watch your habits; for they become your character. Watch your character for it will become your destiny."* ~Frank Outlaw

- **Set Boundaries!** This has been one of the hardest things for me to do. I always have strived to be nice and kind to others. Boundaries represented being strict and not helping others get or achieve what they want or need. I have found that it is completely opposite. We must take care of ourselves before we can take good care of others. *"You cannot pour from an empty cup."* I now equate boundaries with helping define and set clear expectations so all parties simply know what is expected of them.

- If someone wants to be in your life, they will respect your boundaries!

- Remember, **you are ENOUGH** with God! We must focus on our God-given skills and talents that we have to make our business a success. No one succeeds by doing business alone. Remember, you can always outsource in those areas where you are not skillful and have areas of opportunity.

My Truth

I felt like something was missing. I couldn't put my finger on it. According to the world's standards, I had it all, but it was still an empty feeling inside. I began a journey to fill up all those missing pieces and empty spaces.

This is attempt was made seeking tangible fixes:

1. **Trying to gain acceptance through people.**
2. **Spending time crafting "safe" posts on social media.**
3. **Using trips, food, and clothes to temporarily fill and satisfy my voids.**

Distractions can show up in many forms. We must be intentional daily about avoiding setting goals and doing meaningful tasks daily in order to reach them.

Lesson Learned: What I value gets my resources, time, and energy. If I value my business, I must spend time working on it and not just in it. I must be strategic, disciplined, and intentional about avoiding distractions.

VI

COMMITTING TO
Consistency

"Consistency is not perfection.
It is simply refusing to give up."

Unknown

Pursuit

(your

habits)

Consistent action separates the good from the great, the dreamers from the doers, and the leaders from the followers.

The key word is "consistent!" One of my mentors once told me 50% of success is just showing up. For me, this has been the toughest area to master and commit. When you are your "own" boss, you are responsible for holding yourself accountable for your results. Will you show up on days when you don't have any meetings scheduled, and no one is there to hold you accountable? Will you show up on days when it's raining outside and the bed feels extra comfortable? Will you show up when profits are low, and your projections are off? Will you show up when you feel stuck? Will you show up when family and friends believe you are wasting your time and should just get a "REAL" job? Will you show up when you don't want to? "They say motivation gets you going, but consistency keeps you growing."

It all sounds very easy to commit to when it is something you are passionate about, right? Well, this was one of my biggest areas of opportunity. As a creator, I thrive in a less structured environment. However, to be successful, you must develop a system of repetitive habits that help move you closer to an ultimate goal(s). Most things in life are a numbers game. The more you do them, the better you get at them. In order to master them, you must do them consistently. Most of us have faith and believe that we can be successful. The differentiating factor is usually work ethic. How often and long are you willing to persist in order to achieve your goals and dreams. I have found the secret to growth and success is discipline. We must do the work when we don't feel like doing the work. Faith is important. However, the Bible teaches us that faith without work is dead. Read James 2:14-22.

"FAITH WITHOUT WORKS IS DEAD..."

from James 2:20

When Passion, Pursuit & Planning Merge

When you pursue your dream with passion and a plan, it can lead you to operate in your divine purpose. Being consistent in each of these areas will help you sustain your business and be successful. If either of these areas is off, it's difficult to stay aligned with your purpose.

My Truth

I started strong in this area. Over time I decreased my actual planning hours to focus on more execution that brought in money. I eventually learned that you must be intentional about making time to plan and strategize for your business. If you don't, it will be hard to stay in front of trends and remain relevant. In every job, there will be some duties that you don't like or care much to do. I'm not a big fan of the administrative side of running a business, like sales tax, paying bills, maintenance of supplies, etc.

I recently saw a meme that said we sacrifice for what we love. How in love are you with the pursuit or the journey to accomplish your goals? What are you willing to sacrifice to achieve your goals?

The truth is, I sometimes lack true discipline, focus, and motivation.

The secret I discovered in success is it's not how much you have but how grateful you are with what you have. How well do you use the talents, skills, and abilities that God has entrusted you with to make a difference in your life and lives of others? There is no cookie-cutter or secret sauce to being successful. The good thing about being a unique individual is each of us are able to determine how we define success. Every successful person had to start somewhere. I am not an exception. Going through the process prepares me for more profits and the promise.

Lesson Learned: My common threads for success are gratefulness, making a difference in other's lives, and the commitment not to give up. It is essential to have family and friends to share success with… makes the journey much more enjoyable and satis-fying.

VII

LIVING

Liberated

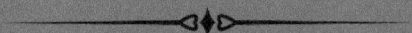

"And you will know the truth, and the truth will make you free."

John 8:32

Pursuit

(your
habits)

I want to go deeper and highlight a few hidden threats that can try to keep you from living your God-given purpose.

Generational Issues

Everyone tends to have family issues and patterns that show up that we deal with at some point in life. We must be intentional about addressing these issues. Once you realize traditions that families have passed down regarded as truths are not relevant; you learn it's okay not to do things the way that your family may have always done them. Just because your mom or grandma did things a certain way, doesn't mean that you have to follow that same pattern or trend. We need to focus on our spiritual, emotional, mental, relational, & financial well-being. This may mean we have to realize that each person is an individual. Our paths are all unique. In a culture that stresses social norms, it is okay to pursue your dreams differently than expected. I've learned that some of the greatest blessings come from following your own path and not being afraid to do things differently.

"Because I am the seed of Abraham, no generational curse can rest upon me" (Galatians 3:29)

Failures/Mistakes

"For though the righteous fall seven times, they rise again, but the wicked stumble when calamity strikes." (Proverbs 24:16)

Many times, mistakes can haunt us longer than they should. It's important to assess failures and mistakes to see the root cause of them. But it is equally important to know how to learn from the mistake and move on. We must be intentional about moving forward and moving on from them. This prevents failure and mistakes from causing us to miss out on our next opportunity.

Lack of Confidence

"God has placed the seed of every living thing within itself. God's ability, enabling me to be all that I can be, is inside of me." (Genesis 1:12)

Failure and mistakes can lead to a lack of confidence. We must be intentional about not letting failures and mistakes hold us back, both profession-ally and personally. I've found the best way to gain confidence is to become a student of learning. Some may call it being a lifelong learner, looking at every experience as a teacher. I have worked on doing things that are outside my comfort zone, as well. This has shown me that I am capable of learning new skills and ways of doing things. In order to evolve, we must be willing to let go of old, ineffective habits and learn new behaviors.

Living liberated is about being intentional in letting go of things that prevent you from being what you define as your highest best self. Liberation focuses on love, truth, and growth. It reminds us that we don't simply improve by living but that we must be purposeful and intentional about it. It reminds us that if we continue to think and do what we have always done, we will get what we have always gotten. Higher-level results require higher-level thinking and purposeful action.

We feel more liberated when we can take responsibility for our actions and happiness. It involves a mental shift of not just finding our value and worth in what other people think of us but in who God has already said we are.

I have learned that happiness is a choice. Even when we feel the most logical response is a negative one, it's up to us to respond with intentionality and positivity. We are human so it's easy to respond in the flesh and not in the spirit. However, we can change our environments and choose positive responses over negative ones.

My Truth

In order to be focused on business, I had to address my issues. It took me a while to find myself again. Early mornings with God, some emotional therapy, and honest conversations helped me get back on track. I had to end some toxic relationships and habits. OH, how this was the hardest part of it all. As humans, we crave routine and familiarity. It's never easy to let go of unhealthy attachments and things. Experiencing God's love and learning self-love have been the most instrumental in me recognizing who I am. When you know true love, it helps you identify the counterfeit. Someone can love you with all their words, but actions are the true sign of someone's love for you. I had to accept all of me...even the ugly pieces that I didn't like: the mistakes, the flaws, the disappointments, the pain.

All of it had to be recognized and embraced, just like all of the good. The sooner we accept that the "negative circumstances" help shape us into the human beings that we want to become, the easier it is to embrace who we really are...beings that appreciate the good because we have witnessed the bad. Beings that gives authentic love because we have experienced hate. Beings that show compassion and grace because we have felt disappointment and pain. It is then and only then, we recognized our true purpose: to thrive and live this life exceedingly, abundantly despite obstacles. I hope you find the courage and the boldness to step out to pursue your God-given purpose while living this life.

You only get this life one time.

Live it to the fullest with no regrets and limit…

BE FREE!

Lesson Learned: It's up to me to break free from self and worldly demands to live my God-given purpose while here on Earth. I am always enough with God. I must position myself during the process to access the promise.

Liberated

Jesus died to give me liberty.

But it's up to me to break free

From what others think about me.

And truly embrace this living spree.

They say nothing good comes easy

But your love for me will never flee.

My trust in you gives me peace

Puts all my fears at ease

I never knew a true love

Till I discovered your grace.

I was drowning in sin

Till you pleaded my case.

So, I've stripped off the pain from fear and rejection

Replaced it with hope, love, and affection.

I've stripped off the mask of lies and deception

Replaced it with peace, life, and redemption.

So, I am no longer what the world calls me

Simply because you set me free.

As I continue to go higher, so God gets the glory

Because finally I'm Liberated!

I started writing this book like most success help books that I have read…sharing my story with candor and transparency – the "normal" inspiring parts of my story. But a change, a "shift" happened in my personal and professional life while writing this.

What I used to value is no longer valuable to me. My taste for fashion and "stuff" changed as well. I started to crave the intangible blessings of life…love, joy, and serenity. I started to appreciate time with family more...the simple things. I asked God to continue to bless me with more life and years here on this Earth, so that I can see my children and grandchildren someday. What I used to pursue is no longer attractive to me.

What was the biggest change?........ I started this journey trying to use my intellect, my connections, and my corporate experience, depending on myself and taking matters into my own hands. I learned quickly. I can only tap into my greatness when I trust in God's strength and promises and not my own! It is about faith in God and patience to be relentless in your pursuit to achieve your unique purpose and dreams, which aligns with God's plan for your life. There is only one you, …which means no one else on this Earth has your unique assignment. Believe in it, love it, own it, and pursue it to the best of your ability.

"And we know that all things work together for good to those who love God, to those who are called according to HIS PURPOSE. For whom He foreknew, He also predestined to be conformed to the image of his Son, that he might be the firstborn among brothers and sisters. And those he predestined, he also called; those he called, he also justified; those he justified, he also glorified." Romans 8:28

Shine

Be careful girl

Life will try to steal yo shine

Hold on tight, because you've got to fight and let it
know…

This little light is mine.

You were made to illuminate like the sun

And not bask in anyone's shade

Remember your purpose & worth

Tell them It's too late!

You got to laugh at those times

When life tries to make you feel less

When it dampened your confidence and courage

Tries to stifle your best

There is so much beauty in growth

And knowing who and whose you are

So shed the insecurities and self-doubt
They won't get you too far!

Stand tall and walk boldly
Be proud of your faith
Don't let regrets treat you coldly
Realize God makes you great!

Be of good courage sis
He has already told you, "He's got this!"
You deserve to live your BEST life on this Earth
In consistent bliss

So know everything will turn out fine.
Just give him the glory & you will SHINE!

THE NEXT
Chapter
MY PLAN VS. GOD'S PLAN

"Commit your work to the LORD, and your plans will be established."

Proverbs 16:3

As my daily interaction changed from just a religious encounter to actually having a relationship with God, my focus changed. I became hungry to know God truly. His love and faithfulness amazed me. I wonder. I sought out to be used by him daily in some form or fashion. Before I knew it, I was being used to serve, testify, pray, and/or teach about his goodness. In the pursuit of purpose, I craved to make a life and not just a living. He set a fire inside of me to be used by him for his work. The purpose I was pursuing became about helping others see their greatness and feel loved and not just my plan for my life. I began to see him in all things throughout the day.

Abundance began to flow easily to me. I trusted him to take care of my life and some. He connected me with the right people at the right time. He blessed me so I'm able to be a blessing. I am a cheerful giver, so the love of money didn't consume me, but money came to me easily. He taught me to trust in him regardless of what my surroundings and circumstances may say. There is so much comfort and peace in knowing no matter what the situation is, God has my back, front, and in-between.

Despite anything that I view as an inadequacy, God can use those areas for his glory. I found that my flaws and weaknesses are where he has the greatest opportunity to work and show himself great. Our strategies and plans can be good. However, when we surrender everything to God, his plan for our lives is greater, bigger, and better. His plan allows us to walk boldly and live the life we are destined to live while using our God-given talents here on Earth.

Destiny Calls

There is peace in answering destiny's call
Letting go and sharing my all
HIS voice is loud and clear
Seek HIM, and HE will stay near

As I pursue the purpose and plan that HE has for me
HE restores and redeems me effortlessly
HE paid the ultimate cost
So I count it all as a gain, never a loss.

When I align with HIS plan for my life
Blessings flow consistently never strife
I become my highest best self
And I'm able to find the joy that never left.

So I'm walking boldly into my Earthly destiny
Because I want to fulfill HIS purpose and plan while
here for me!
So this is just the beginning of my new story
I give all praises to God for HE deserves the glory!

For I know the plans I have for you, declares the LORD, "plans to prosper you and not to harm you, plans to give you hope and a future.

Jeremiah 29:11

BIOGRAPHY
ACKNOWLEDGEMENTS
THINGS TO REMEMBER

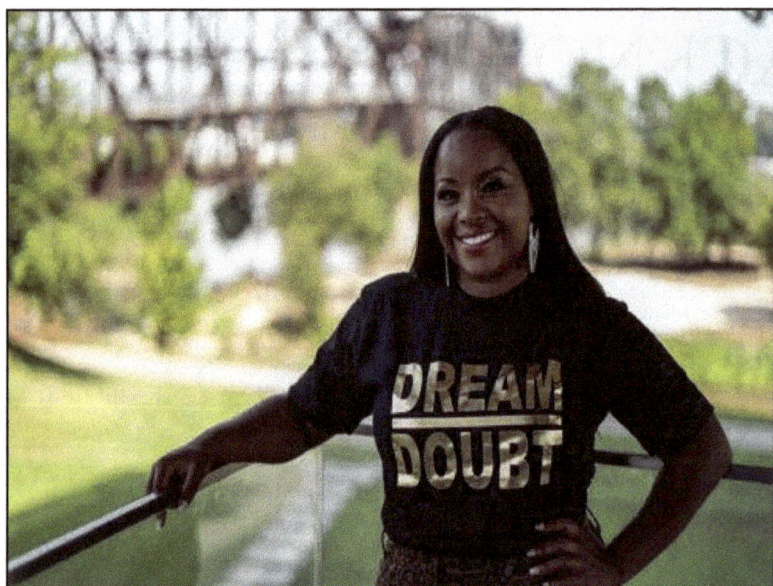

Biography

Ulanda Arnett is a 2002 Agriculture Business Graduate of the University of Arkansas at Pine Bluff and a 2003 Master's Graduate of Agriculture of Economics at the University of Arkansas at Fayetteville. While attending UAPB, Ulanda was a member of the Golden Girls Dance Team, a member of the Agriculture Business Club, Miss Phi Beta Sigma 1999, Miss Junior 2000 – 2001, and Miss UAPB 2001-2002. She is an active member of Alpha Kappa Alpha, Sorority, Inc.

She spent about 13 years in Corporate America, primarily at Tyson Foods, Inc. in Springdale, Arkansas, where she worked in various areas of Human Resources. During her tenure at Tyson Foods, Inc., she was selected in the 2010 class of the NWA's Journal's 40 Under 40 Business Leaders to watch and selected as Business Woman of the Year in 2012.

She has many years of entrepreneurial experience as the Owner of Posh Inspirations (Events & Interior Design Company). She is passionate about helping improve the wealth gap in underserved communities and believes her experience, skills, relationships & love for seeing businesses excel can help with that process.

Acknowledgements

I want to thank my *Lord and Savior Jesus Christ* for divine guidance, purpose, and plans for my life.

I am grateful to my **mother**, Sammia Mae Thomas, my late **father** Charles Arnett, and **stepfather**, Clyde Thomas, for lots of love, lessons, and wisdom.

Thanks to my **daughters**, Charis & Chyloh, who add so much meaning, inspiration, and joy to my life.

Much love and gratitude to my **sisters**, LaTyeshia, Jessica, and Quintina.

Special thanks to a host of **mentors** and **friends** whose journeys inspire and influence me.

Things to Remember

NOTES

Things to Remember

NOTES

_____

_____

_____

_____

_____

_____

_____

_____

_____

_____

_____

_____

_____

_____

_____

_____

_____

_____

_____

_____

_____

_____

Things to Remember

_____

_____

_____

_____

_____

_____

_____

_____

_____

_____

_____

_____

_____

_____

_____

_____

_____

_____

_____

_____

NOTES

_____

_____

_____

_____

_____

_____

_____

_____

_____

_____

_____

_____

_____

_____

_____

_____

_____

_____

_____

_____

Things to Remember

_____

_____

_____

_____

_____

_____

_____

_____

_____

_____

_____

_____

_____

_____

_____

_____

_____

_____

_____

_____

NOTES

Things to Remember

_____

_____

_____

_____

_____

_____

_____

_____

_____

_____

_____

_____

_____

_____

_____

_____

_____

_____

_____

_____

NOTES

_____

_____

_____

_____

_____

_____

_____

_____

_____

_____

_____

_____

_____

_____

_____

_____

_____

_____

_____

www.ingramcontent.com/pod-product-compliance
Lightning Source LLC
Chambersburg PA
CBHW070124100426
42744CB00010B/1911

* 9 7 8 1 9 4 4 1 1 0 3 9 0 *